Handbook of the
Mr. and Mrs. John D. Rockefeller 3rd Collection

THE ASIA SOCIETY

Gallery hours:
Tuesday through Saturday, 10 a.m. to 5 p.m.;
Sunday, 12 noon to 5 p.m.; Thursday, until 8:30 p.m.

Closed Mondays, Christmas Day, and New Year's Day

Design by Roberta Savage
Typesetting by Concept Typographic Services, Inc.
Printed by Eastern Press, Inc.

LIBRARY OF CONGRESS CATALOGUING IN PUBLICATION DATA

Asia Society.
    Handbook of the Mr. and Mrs. John D. Rockefeller 3rd
Collection.

    1. Art, Asian—Catalogs. 2. Rockefeller, John D.,
1906-   —Art collections—Catalogs. 3. Rockefeller,
Blanchette Hooker, 1909-   —Art collections—Catalogs.
I. Title.
N7262.A87 1981   709'.5'07401471   81-7905
ISBN 0-87848-059-5 (pbk.)   AACR2

CONTENTS

INTRODUCTION

This handbook illustrates and describes the Mr. and Mrs. John D. Rockefeller 3rd Collection which was left to The Asia Society at the time of Mr. Rockefeller's death in 1978. Its publication is occasioned by the opening of the permanent collection gallery in the newly constructed headquarters of The Asia Society. In this book, the entire collection is presented to the public for the first time. As it will not be possible to display it in its entirety in a single installation, the handbook serves as an invaluable reference to the full extent of our holdings.

Although the collection has now entered the public domain, by its nature it remains a private one, very much reflecting the personal tastes of Mr. and Mrs. Rockefeller. It is not by any means a survey of Asian art, but is a carefully selected group of objects of uniformly high quality, gathered together over a quarter of a century and giving evidence of a deep appreciation and understanding of the peoples and cultures of Asia.

Mr. Rockefeller began to collect Asian art seriously in 1951, following a trip to Japan. He and his wife made many visits to the Orient over the next twenty-five years, traveling to almost all the countries of Asia. In assembling their collection, they wished to be reminded of their travels and the people they had met, but they also sought to bring together a group of objects that would reveal the extraordinary achievements of Asian artists. Mr. Rockefeller once spoke of his preference for simplicity and directness of statement, and remarked that a piece must "stir and lift" him before he would consider adding it to his collection.

In 1963 Mr. Rockefeller asked Sherman E. Lee, the distinguished scholar of Asian art and director of The Cleveland Museum of Art, to advise him. From that time, Dr. Lee was able to bring a number of important pieces to Mr. and Mrs. Rockefeller's attention, although, of course, the decision as to what would finally be acquired was made by the collectors themselves. Dr. Lee also served as guest curator for the two exhibitions of selections from the collection that were shown at The Asia Society in 1970 and 1975.

One clearly stated wish of Mr. Rockefeller's was that the collection always remain small and of intimate scale. At the same time, he wanted it to be a living part of The Asia Society, and accordingly he provided a modest endowment for acquisitions. He also expressed the hope that gifts of objects from other donors might be added to the Society's collection as well. One such gift has already been made and another committed. There are also sev-

eral pieces included here which have been retained by Mrs. Rockefeller but are designated as bequests to the Society in her will.

The handbook entries have been written by Robert D. Mowry, the newly appointed curator of the collection. Part of his information was drawn from the 1970 and 1975 catalogues written by Sherman Lee and from the records that were meticulously maintained by Bertha Saunders, who cared for the collection before it came to the Society. The photographs are by Otto E. Nelson, who has now been working with this collection and The Asia Society for twenty-one years. Once again, we thank him for his tireless, painstaking efforts. Sarah Bradley, the Gallery's assistant director, supervised the production of the handbook. Mary Ellen T. Gilroy, department assistant, provided invaluable organizational support.

It is our hope one day to publish a scholarly catalogue raisonné of this collection. Meanwhile, this publication and the display of the objects themselves in the Mr. and Mrs. John D. Rockefeller 3rd Gallery will serve to reveal the extraordinary nature of the great and lasting gift Mr. and Mrs. Rockefeller have made to us all.

Allen Wardwell

SOUTH ASIA

Railing Pillar with a Female Figure Under an Ashoka Tree

India, Mathura area; Kushan period, late 2nd-3rd century
Mottled red sandstone; H. 30¾ in.
1979.1

Head of Buddha

Pakistan, Gandhara area; Kushan period, late 2nd-3rd century
Gray schist; H. 14½ in.
1979.2

Buddha

Pakistan, Gandhara area; Kushan period,
    2nd-3rd century, the face recut in recent
    times
Gray schist; H. 72 in.
1979.3

Kneeling Figure

Afghanistan, probably Hadda; 4th-5th
    century
Stucco with traces of polychromy; H. 12⅛ in.
1979.4

The Buddha Shakyamuni

India, Sarnath area; Gupta period, ca. 475
Grayish buff sandstone; H. 34⅛ in.
1979.5

Rama and Lakshmana

India, Uttar Pradesh, Bhitargaon (?); Gupta period, 5th century
Reddish buff earthenware; H. 17½ in., W. (at base) 16¾ in.
1979.6

The Buddha Shakyamuni in Abhaya-mudra

North India; Gupta period, first half 6th century
Bronze; H. 27 in.
1979.8

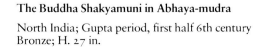

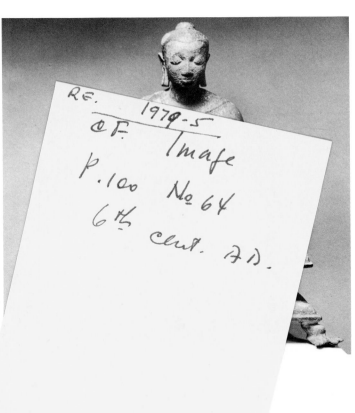

9

The Buddha Shakyamuni in Abhaya-mudra

North India; Gupta period, late 6th century
Bronze; H. 19⅜ in.
1979.9

The Bodhisattva Avalokiteshvara

India, Bihar; Gupta period, ca. 600
Black schist; H. 77 in.
1979.10

Tirthankara Rishabhanatha

India; 6th-8th century
Bronze; H. 10½ in.
1979.11

Tirthankara

Central India; 7th-8th century
Bronze; H. 11 in.
1979.12

Ten-armed Ganesha

Central India; 8th century
Dark brown sandstone; H. 49½ in.
1979.13

Uma-Maheshvara-murti (Shiva and Parvati)

Central or West India; 9th century
Bronze; H. 5¼ in.
1979.14

Buddha in Abhayavara-mudra

South India, Tamil Nadu, Nagapattinam area;
    8th-10th century
Bronze; H. 27¼ in.
1979.15

Seated Queen (?)

South India, Pandya area; Pallava period, 8th-9th century
Buff granite; H. 67 in., W. 34¾ in.
1979.16

Vishnu

South India; Pallava period, 8th century
Bronze; H. 13¼ in.
1979.17

Goddess

South India; Pallava or Eastern Chalukya
    period, 8th-9th century
Bronze; H. 12 in.
1979.18

Parvati

South India, Pandya area (?); transitional, Pallava to Chola period, ca. 9th-10th century
Bronze; H. 35 in.
1979.19

Shiva Nataraja (Shiva as Lord of the Dance)

South India, Tamil Nadu, Tanjavur District; Chola period, late 10th-early 11th century
Bronze; H. 26¾ in.
1979.20

Parvati

South India, Tamil Nadu; Chola period,
    mid-10th century
Bronze; H. 31¾ in.
1979.21

Kaliyahimarddaka Krishna (Krishna Dancing
    on Kaliya)

South India, Tamil Nadu; Chola period,
    10th-11th century
Bronze; H. 34½ in.
1979.22

Rama

South India, Tamil Nadu; Chola period, early
    11th century
Reportedly excavated in the Tanjore area
Bronze; H. 37¾ in.
1979.23

Balakrishna (Dancing Krishna)

South India, Tamil Nadu; Chola period,
  11th century
Reportedly excavated from Tiruvan
  Vanpanalur Temple
Bronze; H. 18⅞ in.
1979.24

Brahma

South India, Tamil Nadu; Chola period,
  11th century
Bronze; H. 15⅝ in.
1979.25

Ganesha

South India, Tamil Nadu; Chola period,
  ca. 11th century
Bronze; H. 21¼ in., W. (at base) 10¾ in.
1979.26

Mannikkavachaka (Saintly Disciple of Shiva)

South India, Tamil Nadu; Chola period,
    11th century
Reportedly excavated from Tiruvan
    Vanpanalur Temple
Bronze; H. 19¼ in.
1979.27

Somaskanda-murti (Shiva and Parvati, originally with a figure of their son, Skanda)

South India, Tamil Nadu; Chola period, late 11th century
Bronze; H. 19 in., W. (at base) 23¾ in.
1979.28

Shiva Nataraja (Shiva as Lord of the Dance)

South India, Tamil Nadu; Chola period, 12th century
Bronze; H. 29¼ in.
1979.29

Nandi (Vehicle of Shiva)

South India, Tamil Nadu; ca. 1250-1300
Bronze; H. 20¼ in., L. 20½ in.
1979.30

Celestial Musician

South India, Mysore; Hoysala period, 13th century
Brownish gray stone; H. 39¾ in.
1979.31

Surasundari (Celestial Beauty)

India, Rajasthan; Chandella period, 10th
century
Red sandstone; H. 19½ in.
1979.32

Surasundari (Celestial Beauty)

India, Rajasthan; Chandella period, 11th
century
Red sandstone; H. 21¼ in.
1979.33

Birth of Parshvanatha (?)

India, Rajasthan; Chandella period, 11th
century
Cream sandstone; H. 12½ in., W. 23 in.
1979.34

The Bodhisattva Manjushri Seated on Lion Vehicle

India, Bengal; Pala period, 9th century
Gilt bronze with inlays of silver and copper; H. 5½ in.
1979.35

Stele with Crowned Buddha in Bhumisparsa-mudra

India; Pala period, 10th century
Gray chlorite; H. 27¾ in.
1979.36

Stele with Buddha in Bhumisparsa-mudra

India; Pala period, 10th century
Black chlorite; H. 28¼ in.
1979.37

The Bodhisattva Tara

India; Pala period, 10th century
Buff sandstone or conglomerate stone with
    polychromy and gilding; H. 3¾ in.,
    W. (at base) 2⅛ in.
1979.38

Stele with Khasarpana-Lokeshvara

India, Bengal; Pala period, late 10th–early 11th
    century
Black chlorite; H. 54¾ in.
1979.39

Stele with Lokeshvara

India, Orissa; Pala period, 10th-11th century
Gray chlorite; H. 37½ in.
1979.40

Four-armed Lokeshvara

Sri Lanka; 6th-8th century
Bronze; H. 8¾ in.
1979.41

**Stele with Figures Adoring the Buddha
    Shakyamuni in Meditation**

Kashmir; 8th-9th century
Ivory; H. 3⅞ in., W. 2⅞ in
1979.42

Vishnu

Kashmir; 8th-9th century
Brass; H. 13½ in.
1979.43

Crowned Buddha Shakyamuni in Dharmachakra-mudra

Kashmir; 8th-early 9th century
Brass with inlays of copper, silver, and zinc(?) and with an inscription
    which translates "This is the pious gift of the devout Shankarasena,
    the great Lord of the elephant brigade, and of the pure-minded and
    pious Devashriya, made in the second day of Vaishakha in the year
    3 [or 8];" H. 12¼ in.
1979.44

23

The Bodhisattva Padmapani

Kashmir; 9th century
Brass with inlays of copper and silver;
    H. 27¼ in.
1979.45

A Bodhisattva, probably Manjushri

North India or Nepal; 12th-13th century
Brass inlaid with turquoise; H. 12⅜ in.
1979.46

The Bodhisattva Avalokiteshvara

Nepal; ca. 10th century
Gilt copper with inlays of semi-precious
    stones; H. 26¾ in.
1979.47

Uma-Maheshvara-murti (Shiva and Parvati)

Nepal; late 10th-early 11th century
Bronze; H. 6 in., W. 6¼ in.
1979.48

A Bodhisattva, probably Avalokiteshvara

Nepal; 13th century
Gilt copper with inlays of semi-precious stones; H. 18¾ in.
1979.49

The Bodhisattva Avalokiteshvara

Nepal; 13th-14th century
Gilt bronze; H. 11 in.
1979.50

The Bodhisattva Avalokiteshvara

Nepal; 15th-16th century
Gilt bronze; H. 17 in.
1979.51

The Bodhisattva Tara (Saptara Lochana)

Nepal; 17th century
Silver with inlays of copper and semi-precious
    stones; H. 6¾ in.
1979.52

Four Leaves from a Manuscript of the Astasahasrika Prajnaparamita *(Book of Transcendental Wisdom)*

Nepal; 12th century
Manuscript leaves; ink and color on palm leaf; H. 3 in., W. 17¼ in.
1979.53.1-4

Four Leaves from a Manuscript of the Gandavyuha *(Structure of the World)*

Nepal; 12th century
Manuscript leaves; ink and color on palm leaf; H. 2 in., W. 21½ in.
1979.54.1-4

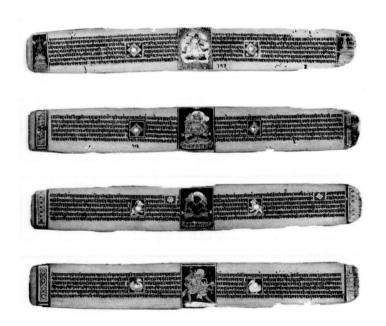

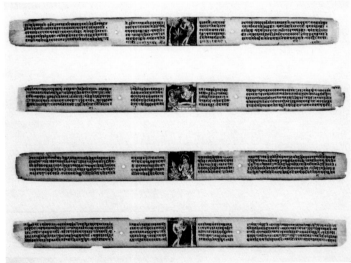

Illuminated Page from a Manuscript of the Bhagavata Purana

India, Southern Rajasthan, probably Mewar; Rajput School, ca. 1550
Manuscript page; ink and color on paper; H. 7 in., W. 9 in.
1979.55

Illuminated Page from a Manuscript of the Ta'rikh-i-alfi *(History of a Thousand Years)*

India; Mughal School, reign of Akbar, ca. 1582-1596
Manuscript page; ink and color on paper; H. 16 in., W. 8⅝ in.
1979.56

Abhisarika Nayaka (A Heroine Comes to her Lover Through the Rain)

India; Malwa School, ca. 1630
Manuscript page; ink and color on paper; H. 9 in., W. 6⅝ in.
1979.57

Gopis Searching for Krishna in the Night

India, Rajasthan; 17th century
Temple hanging *(pichhavais);* polychromy,
gold, and silver on dyed cotton;
H. 80¾ in., W. 86½ in.
1979.59

**Illuminated Page from a Manuscript of the
Amaru Sataka**

India; Rajput School, ca. 1660
Manuscript page; ink and color on paper;
H. 8¼ in., W. 5¾ in.
1979.58

Gopis in the Woods

India, Rajasthan, Bundi; late 18th century
Temple hanging *(pichhavais);* polychromy on
dyed cotton; H. 74 in., W. 118 in.
1979.60

SOUTHEAST ASIA

Uma (Manifestation of Parvati)

Cambodia; Pre-Angkor period, late 7th
  century
Reportedly from Kompong Khleang
Gray sandstone; H. 15 in.
1979.61

Head of Vishnu

Cambodia; Pre-Angkor period, 7th-8th
  century
Gray sandstone; H. 16¾ in.
1979.62

The Bodhisattva Maitreya

Cambodia; Pre-Angkor period, ca. late 8th
  century
Recovered at Pra Kon Chai, Thailand; style of
  Kompong Preah
Bronze with inlays of silver and black stone;
  H. 38 in.
1979.63

31

Shiva

Cambodia; Angkor period, second half 10th century
Transitional style between Koh Ker and Baphuon
Gray sandstone; H. 41 in.
1979.64

Female Figure, perhaps Uma

Cambodia; Angkor period, first quarter 11th century
Style of Baphuon
Gray sandstone; H. 38 in.
1979.65

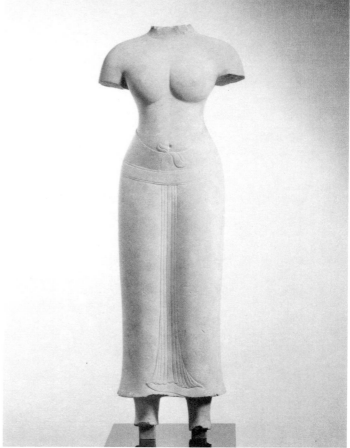

Male Figure

Cambodia; Angkor period, third quarter 11th century
Style of Baphuon
Greenish gray sandstone; H. 41½ in.
1979.66

Vajrasattva

Cambodia; Angkor period, first half 12th century
Style of Angkor Vat
Bronze; H. 5 in.
1979.67

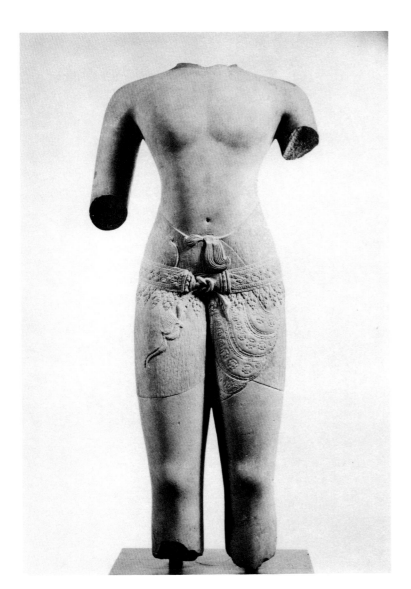

Crowned Buddha Seated in Meditation and Sheltered by Mucilinda

Cambodia; Angkor period, first half 12th century
Style of Angkor Vat
Bronze with recent covering of black and gold lacquer and gold leaf;
   H. 28¾ in.
  1979.68 a-c

Kneeling Woman

Cambodia; Angkor period, 11th-12th century
Transitional style between Baphuon and Angkor Vat
Bronze; H. 18¾ in.
1979.69

Palanquin Fittings

Cambodia; Angkor period, 12th century
Style of Angkor Vat
Bronze; Hooks, H. 9 in., Ring, H. 6 in.
1979.70.1-3

Head of Buddha

Cambodia; Angkor period, 12th-13th century
Style of Angkor Thom: Bayon
Grayish buff sandstone; H. 13 in.
1979.71

Pair of Standing Royal Figures

Cambodia; Angkor period, late 12th-early 13th century
Style of Angkor Thom: Bayon
Grayish buff sandstone; H. (male) 54 in., H. (female) 55 in.
1979.72.1-2

Kneeling Male Worshipper

Thailand; Sri Deb style, first half 7th century
Reportedly from Sri Deb
Gray sandstone with brown markings;
    H. 26⅞ in.
1979.73

Buddha in Vitarka-mudra

Thailand; Mon-Dvaravati period, 7th-8th
    century
Bronze; H. 9⅛ in.
1979.74

Buddha

Thailand; Mon-Dvaravati period, late 7th-8th
    century
Gray limestone with traces of gilding;
    H. 36½ in.
1979.75

Head of Buddha

Thailand; Mon-Dvaravati period, ca. 8th century
Gray limestone; H. 27 in.
1979.76

Stele with Buddha and Two Attendants

Thailand; Mon-Dvaravati period, 8th century
Grayish green sandstone; H. 16⅝ in.
1979.77

Head of Buddha

Thailand; Mon-Dvaravati period, ca. 8th
  century
Stucco; H. 6 in.
1979.78

Head of a Woman

Thailand; Mon-Dvaravati period, ca. 7th-8th
  century
Stucco; H. 7¼ in.
1979.79

Lokeshvara

South Thailand; Shrivijaya period, 7th-8th
  century
Bronze; H. 4⅝ in.
1979.81

Crowned Buddha in Abhaya-mudra

Thailand; Lopburi style, 12th-13th century
Reportedly recovered near Pimai
Bronze; H. 9¼ in.
1979.80

The Bodhisattva Manjushri on a Lion Throne

Indonesia, Java; Shrivijaya period, late 8th
   century
Reportedly excavated at Nakorn Rajshima
Bronze; H. 12¼ in., W. (at base) 6⅛ in.
1979.82

The Bodhisattva Maitreya

Indonesia, Java; Shrivijaya period, 8th-9th
   century
Bronze; H. 18 in.
1979.83

The Bodhisattva Prajnaparamita

Indonesia, Java; Shrivijaya period, 9th
   century
Bronze; H. 6¼ in.
1979.84

Head of Buddha

Indonesia, Java; Central Javanese period, ca. early 9th century
From Borobudur
Gray andalite; H. 13 in.
1979.85

Head of the Bodhisattva Avalokiteshvara

Indonesia, Java; Central Javanese period, 9th century
Possibly from Borobudur or Chandi Sewu
Gray lava stone; H. 21¼ in.
1979.86

Four Vajra-Bodhisattvas

Indonesia, East Java; 8th-9th century
Perhaps from Ngandjuk (Kediri)
Bronze; H. (average) 3 ¼ in.
1979.87.1-4

Vajrasattva

Indonesia, East Java; 11th-12th century
Gray volcanic stone; H. 41½ in.
1979.88

The Buddha Shakyamuni in Bhumisparsa-mudra

Burma; 11th century
Brass and copper; H. 5⅝ in.
1979.89

The Buddha Shakyamuni in Bhumisparsa-mudra with
    Kneeling Worshippers

Burma; 14th-15th century
Gilt bronze; H. 16 in., W. (at base) 14¾ in.
1979.91 a-c

Stele with Scenes from the Life of the Buddha

Burma or Northeast India, possibly
    Bodhgaya; 12th-early 13th century
Sandstone with traces of gilding and with the
    syllable *om* inscribed on the reverse in
    Tibetan; H. 7¾ in., W. (at base) 4½ in.
1979.90

Vase

Thailand; 14th-15th century
Sawankhalok ware: light gray stoneware with incised decoration
    under celadon glaze; H. 8⅛ in., Diam. 7¾ in.
1979.92

Covered Jar

Thailand; 14th-15th century
Excavated at Sulawesi, Philippines
Sawankhalok ware: light gray stoneware with incised decoration
    under celadon glaze; H. (including cover)) 6 in., Diam. 4½ in.
1979.93 a, b

Kendi (Spouted Jar)

Thailand; 14th-15th century
Sawankhalok ware: light gray stoneware with
 incised decoration under celadon glaze;
 H. 5¾ in., Diam. 6¼ in.
1979.94

Storage Jar

Thailand; 14th-16th century
Excavated at Kamphaeng Phet, Thailand
Kalong ware: light gray stoneware with
 incised and appliqué decoration under
 celadon glaze; H. 17⅞ in., Diam. 14¼ in.
1979.95

45

Storage Jar with Floral Decoration

Vietnam; 14th-15th century
Buff stoneware with incised decoration under caramel-colored glaze;
    H. 13⅛ in., Diam. 12 in.
1979.96

Bowl with Peony Decoration

Vietnam; 15th century
Annamese blue-and-white ware: porcelaneous white stoneware with
    underglaze decoration in cobalt blue; H. 2⅝ in., Diam. 9⅝ in.
1979.97

46

Ewer in the Shape of a Duck

Vietnam; 15th century
Annamese blue-and-white ware: porcelaneous white stoneware with
    underglaze decoration in cobalt blue; H. 5¾ in., L. 8 in.
1979.99

Storage Jar with Scrolling Peony Decoration

Vietnam; 15th century
Annamese blue-and-white ware: porcelaneous white stoneware with
    underglaze decoration in cobalt blue; H. 13⅛ in., Diam. 14 in.
1979.98 a, b

47

CHINA

Ritual Wine Vessel Type Yu with Bovine and T'ao-t'ieh Decoration

China; Early Western Chou period, ca. late 11th century B.C.
Bronze, the body and the cover each with a cast inscription reading *Fu Ting Hsi* (Father Ting Sacrificial Buffalo); H. (including handle) 14⅞ in., Diam. (across flanges) 8¾ in.
1979.100 a, b

Ritual Wine Vessel Type Yu

China; Early Western Chou period, ca. late 11th-early 10th century B.C.
Bronze, the body and the cover each with a cast inscription reading *Fu Kuei* (Father Kuei); H. (including handles) 12⅝ in., Diam. (across handle attachments) 9½ in.
1979.101 a, b

Ritual Food Vessel Type Kuei with T'ao-t'ieh Decoration

China; Early Western Chou period, ca. late 11th-early 10th century B.C.
Bronze with a cast inscription reading *Tso Pao I* ([I] made [this] precious *i* [vessel]); H. 7½ in., Diam. (across handles) 12¼ in.
1979.102

Ritual Food Vessel Type Kuei

China; Early Eastern Chou period, ca. 6th century B.C.
Reportedly excavated at Lin-tzu, Shantung province
Bronze; H. (including cover) 12¾ in., Diam. (across handles) 15½ in.
1979.103 a, b

Wine Vessel Type Pien-hu with Stamped Decoration

China; Late Eastern Chou period, 5th-3rd century B.C.
Bronze inlaid with copper; H. 14½ in., W. 13¾ in.
1979.104

Chariot Fitting with Tiger Clasp

China; Late Eastern Chou period, 5th-3rd century B.C.
Bronze inlaid with silver; L. 7⅛ in.
1979.105 a, b

Standing Horse

China; Late Eastern Chou to Han period, 3rd century B.C.-3rd century A.D.
Ordos style
Bronze; H. 2⅜ in., L. 2⅛ in.
1979.106

Wine Warming Vessel Type Tsun with Stylized Landscape Decoration

China; Western Han period (206 B.C.-A.D. 9)
Gilt bronze; H. 6¼ in., Diam. (at mouth) 8¼ in.
1979.107

Large Basin Type P'an with Animal Decoration

China; Western Han period (206 B.C.-A.D. 9)
Bronze core enveloped with sheet silver, the silver engraved and gilded; Diam. 20 in.
1979.108

Po-shan Lu (Censer in the Shape of Mt. Po)

China; Eastern Han period, ca. 2nd century
Gilt bronze; H. 5½ in., Diam. (of saucer) 4⅝ in.
1979.109 a, b

Tomb Figure Representing a Male Attendant

China; Han Dynasty (206 B.C.-A.D. 220)
Gray earthenware with white slip and traces of polychromy;
    H. 21¼ in.
1979.110

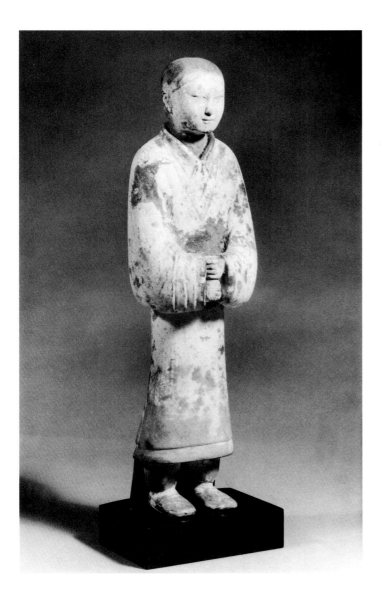

Crouching Pi-hsieh Chimera

China; Six Dynasties period (220-589)
Gilt bronze; H. 1½ in.; L. 3⅝ in.
1979.111

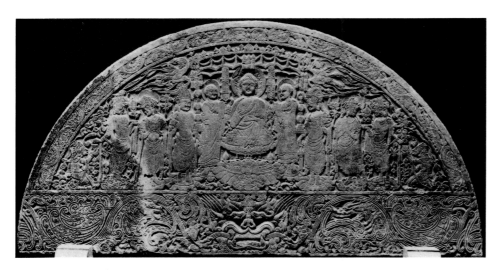

Tympanum with Relief Showing the Buddha Shakyamuni Preaching at Vulture Peak

China; Six Dynasties period, Northern Ch'i (550-577)
Gray stone; H. 35 in., W. 70 in.
1979.112

Tomb Figure Representing a Court Lady with Cymbals

China; T'ang dynasty, 8th century
"Three-color" *(san-ts'ai)* ware: white earthenware with variegated lead glaze and with traces of polychromy on the face and hair; H. 14⅛ in.
1979.113

Tomb Figure Representing a Civil Official

China; T'ang dynasty, 8th century
"Three-color" *(san-ts'ai)* ware: white earthenware with variegated lead glaze and with traces of polychromy on the face, hair, and cap; H. 40¾ in.
1979.114

Head of a Bodhisattva, perhaps Ta Shih-chih
(The Bodhisattva Mahasthamaprapta)

China; T'ang to Northern Sung period, ca. 9th-10th century
Light gray stone with traces of polychromy; H. 13 in.
1979.115

Bowl with Landscape and Floral Decoration

China; T'ang dynasty, ca. 7th-early 8th century
Silver with engraving and gilding and with the lotus petal motif
 worked in repoussé; H. 2¾ in., Diam. 6⅞ in.
1979.117

Lobed Dish with Foliate Rim and Landscape Decoration

China; Six Dynasties to Sui period, ca. 6th century
Gilt silver with decoration worked in repoussé; H. ¾ in., Diam.
 (across points) 4⅞ in.
1979.116

Footed Cup with Bird and Flower Decoration

China; T'ang dynasty, ca. 7th-early 8th century
Silver with engraving and with the lotus petal motif worked in
    repoussé; H. 1⅞ in., Diam. 2½ in.
1979.118

Jade Pi-hsieh Chimera

China; Sung to Ch'ing dynasty, 12th-19th century
Sea-green nephrite mottled with brown and black; H. 7¾ in., L. 12 in.
1979.120

Mirror with Bird and Flower Decoration

China; T'ang dynasty, ca. 8th century
Reportedly excavated in Honan province
Bronze with gold and silver inlays in lacquer *(heidatsu* technique);
    H. 5⅞ in., W. 5⅞ in.
1979.119

Recumbent Horse

China; Yüan to Ming dynasty, ca. 14th-early 15th century
Wood with brushed brown lacquer; H. 8 in., L. 14¾ in.
1979.121

Lobed Dish with Landscape Decoration

China; Ming dynasty, early 15th century (probably Yung-lo period,
    1403-1424)
Carved cinnabar lacquer on wood or cloth and with an inscription
    reading *Ta Ming Yung-lo nien chih* incised on the base; H. 1⅝ in.,
    Diam. 13⅝ in.
1979.122

Figures in a Mountain Landscape

Attributed to Lou Kuan (active, ca. 1265-1274)
China; Southern Sung to Yüan period, late 13th-14th
    century
Hanging scroll; ink and slight color on silk and with signa-
    ture reading *Ch'ien-t'ang Lou Kuan;* H. 69 in.,
    W. 34¾ in.
1979.123

Landscapes in the Manner of Old Masters

By Kuan Ssu (active, ca. 1590-1630)
China; Ming dynasty
Album of ten leaves; ink and light color on paper; H. 10¾ in., W. 7⅛ in.
Gift of Robert H. Ellsworth in memory of John D. Rockefeller 3rd
1980.1.1-10

天啓丁卯
季春之望
君白謝士
開思寫於
霞幕山房

59

Temple on a Mountain Ledge

By K'un-ts'an (also called Shih-ch'i; 1612-ca. 1686)
China; Ch'ing dynasty, dated 1661
Hanging scroll; ink and color on paper and with signature reading *Chieh-ch'iu Shih-tao-jen chi-hsieh*; H. 33½ in., W. 19 in.
1979.124

Storage Jar with Spiral Decoration

China; Neolithic period, ca. 2200 B.C.
Yang-shao culture, Pan-shan type
Buff earthenware with decoration in red and black slips; H. 15⅝ in., Diam. (without handles) 13¾ in.
1979.125

Covered Jar

China; Six Dynasties period, Western Chin, ca. early 4th century
Yüeh type ware: light gray stoneware with impressed and appliqué decoration under celadon glaze; H. (with cover) 10⅞ in., Diam. 10 in.
1979.126 a, b

Storage Jar with Animal Masks and Floral Medallions

China; Sui dynasty (581-618)
Buff earthenware with appliqué decoration under green lead glaze; H. 16⅝ in., Diam. 13½ in.
1979.127

Footed Dish with Cloud and Floral Decoration

China; T'ang dynasty, 8th century
"Three-color" *(san-ts'ai)* ware: white earthenware with stamped decoration under variegated lead glaze; H. 2⅛ in., Diam. 9½ in.
1979.128

Cha-tou Jar (Cuspidor?)

China; T'ang dynasty, ca. 9th century
Light gray stoneware with brownish black glaze and with remains of a brush-written inscription dated to 841; H. 4⅜ in., Diam. 6¼ in.
1979.129

Wide-mouthed Jar

China; T'ang to Northern Sung period, 8th-
11th century
Grayish buff stoneware with greenish brown
glaze; H. 9⅝ in., Diam. 11 in.
1979.130

Cusped Bowl with Peony Decoration

China; Northern Sung period, ca. early 12th
century
Northern Celadon ware, probably from
Yao-chou or Lin-ju: light gray stoneware
with carved, combed, and incised decoration under celadon glaze; H. 2¾ in.,
Diam. 6 in.
1979.131

Dish with Peony Decoration

China; Northern Sung period, ca. early 12th
century
Northern Celadon ware, probably from
Yao-chou: light gray stoneware with
carved and combed decoration under
celadon glaze; H. 1½ in., Diam. 7 in.
1979.132

Two Bowls with Flower and Wave Decoration

China; Chin period, 12th century
Northern Celadon ware, probably from
Yao-chou: light gray stoneware with
carved and combed decoration under
celadon glaze; H. 2⅛ in., Diam. 5⅜ in.
1979.133 and 1979.134

Bowl with Stylized Floral Decoration

China; Chin period, 12th century
Northern Celadon ware, probably from
Yao-chou: light gray stoneware with
carved decoration under celadon glaze;
H. 2½ in., Diam. 4 in.
1979.135

Bowl with Stylized Floral Decoration

China; Chin period, 12th century
Northern Celadon ware, probably from
Yao-chou: light gray stoneware with
incised decoration under celadon glaze and
with brush-written inscription dated to
1162; H. 4½ in., Diam. 8 in.
1979.136

Cup

China; Northern Sung to Chin period, ca. 12th century
Chün ware: light gray stoneware with light blue glaze and with purple
 suffusions from copper filings; H. 1¾ in., Diam. 3⅜ in.
1979.137

Hsi Brushwasher with Ring Handle

China; Northern Sung to Yüan period, 11th-13th century
Chün ware: light gray stoneware with light blue glaze; H. 2¼ in.,
 Diam. 6¾ in.
1979.138

Bowl with Lotus Decoration

China; Northern Sung period, 11th-early 12th century
Ting ware: porcelain with incised decoration under honey-colored
 glaze, the rim bound with copper; H. 2½ in., Diam. 8¾ in.
1979.139

Dish with Dragon Decoration

China; Northern Sung period, early 12th century
Ting ware: porcelain with impressed decoration under honey-colored
  glaze; H. 2 in., Diam. 9 in.
1979.140

Mei-p'ing Jar

China; Northern Sung to Chin period, 12th century
Tz'u-chou ware, probably from Hsiu-wu or Tz'u-chou: light gray
  stoneware with sgraffito designs in black slip on white slip under
  transparent glaze; H. 12½ in., Diam. 8½ in.
1979.141

Vase with Peony Decoration

China; Northern Sung to Chin period, 12th century
Tz'u-chou ware, probably from Hsiu-wu or Tz'u-chou: grayish buff
    stoneware with sgraffito decoration in black slip on white slip
    under transparent green lead glaze; H. 8⅛ in., Diam. 3⅝ in.
1979.142

Truncated Bottle

China; Northern Sung period, 11th-early 12th century
Northern black ware of the Tz'u-chou family: grayish buff stoneware
    decorated with appliqué clay ribs and brown slip glaze under black
    glaze; H. 8⅛ in., Diam. 7¾ in.
1979.143

Hsi Brushwasher with "Oil-spot" Decoration

China; Northern Sung period, 11th-early 12th century
Northern black ware of the Tz'u-chou family: light gray stoneware
    with black glaze and irridescent iron spots; H. 2⅝ in., Diam.
    6½ in.
1979.144

Tea Bowl with Floral Decoration

China; Sung dynasty, 11th-13th century
Chien ware: purplish brown stoneware with black glaze marked with
    "hare's fur" streaks and with decoration in overglaze iron brown
    slip, the rim bound with silver; H. 2⅞ in., Diam. 4⅞ in.
1979.145

Censer

China; Southern Sung period, 12th-13th century
Kuan ware, *Ko* type: black stoneware with grayish blue, crackled
    glaze; H. 3¼ in., Diam. (at mouth) 4⅝ in.
1979.146

Leaf-shaped Cup

China; Southern Sung to Yüan period, 13th century
Kuan type ware: gray stoneware with grayish green glaze; H. 1⅜ in.,
    Diam. (across points) 3⅝ in.
1979.147

Jar with Floral Decoration

China; Southern Sung to Yüan period, 13th-
    early 14th century
Ch'ing-pai (ying-ch'ing) ware: porcelain with
    incised and carved decoration under light
    blue glaze; H. 6½ in., Diam. 6⅛ in.
1979.149

Large Dish with Stylized Floral Decoration

China; Yüan dynasty (1279-1368)
Lung-ch'üan celadon ware: light gray stoneware with impressed deco-
    ration under celadon glaze; H. 3½ in., Diam. 16½ in.
1979.148

Large Dish

China; Yüan dynasty, 14th century
Ching-te-chen white porcelain; the name Shah Jahan (1593-1666) incised into the glaze on the exterior and the weight incised on the unglazed base; H. 3½ in., Diam. 17⅜ in.
1979.150

Large Dish with Ch'i-lin Decoration

China; Yüan dynasty, second half 14th century
Ching-te-chen blue-and-white ware: porcelain with underglaze decoration in cobalt blue and with an inscription reading *Shah Jahan Ibn' Jahangir Shah, 1063* incised on the footring, the date corresponding to 1646; H. 3 in., Diam. 18⅜ in.
1979.151

Cup Stand with Floral Decoration

China; Yüan to Ming dynasty, late 14th century
Ching-te-chen red-and-white ware: porcelain with underglaze decoration in copper red; H. 1 in., Diam. 7¾ in.
1979.152

Flat Dish with Floral Decoration

China; Ming dynasty, late 14th century (probably Hung-wu period, 1368-1398)
Ching-te-chen red-and-white ware: porcelain with underglaze decoration in copper red; H. ¾ in., Diam. 7½ in.
1979.154

Jar with "Three Friends of Winter" Decoration
  (Pine, Plum, and Bamboo)

China; Yüan to Ming dynasty, late 14th century
Ching-te-chen red-and-white ware: porcelain with underglaze decoration in copper red; H. 20 in., Diam. 16¾ in.
1979.153

Ewer with Floral Decoration

China; Ming dynasty, early 15th century (probably Yung-lo period, 1403-1424)
Ching-te-chen white ware: porcelain with incised underglaze decoration; H. 13 in.
1979.155

Hu-lu-p'ing (Gourd-shaped Bottle)

China; Ming dynasty, early 15th century (probably Yung-lo period, 1403-1424)
Ching-te-chen white ware: porcelain with incised underglaze decoration; H. 12½ in., W. 8⅛ in.
1979.156

Foliate Dish with Fruit and Floral Decoration

China; Ming dynasty, early 15th century (probably Yung-lo period,
 1403-1424)
Ching-te-chen white ware: porcelain with incised underglaze decoration; H. 1 in., Diam. 7⅞ in.
1979.157

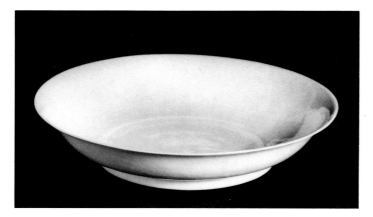

Bowl with Floral Decoration

China; Ming dynasty, early 15th century (probably Yung-lo period,
 1403-1424)
Ching-te-chen white ware: porcelain with incised and impressed
 underglaze decoration; H. 4 in., Diam. 8¼ in.
1979.159

Dish with Dragon and Cloud Decoration

China; Ming dynasty, early 15th century (probably Yung-lo period,
 1403-1424)
Ching-te-chen white ware: eggshell porcelain with impressed underglaze decoration; H. 1¼ in., Diam. 6⅜ in.
1979.158

Flask with Dragon and Floral Decoration

China; Ming dynasty, early 15th century (probably Yung-lo period, 1403-1424)
Ching-te-chen blue-and-white ware: porcelain with underglaze decoration in cobalt blue; H. 18½ in., Diam. 14 in.
1979.160

Bowl with Floral Decoration

China; Ming dynasty, Hsüan-te period (1426-1435)
Ching-te-chen white ware: porcelain with incised underglaze decoration and with mark reading *Ta Ming Hsüan-te nien chih* within a double circle; H. 4 in., Diam. 8⅛ in.
1979.161

Conical Bowl with Fruit and Floral Decoration

China; Ming dynasty, Hsüan-te period (1426-1435)
Ching-te-chen blue-and-white ware: porcelain with underglaze decoration in cobalt blue and with mark reading *Ta Ming Hsüan-te nien chih* within a double circle; H. 3⅛ in., Diam. 8¾ in.
1979.162

Stem Cup with Dragon and Cloud Decoration

China; Ming dynasty, Hsüan-te period (1426-1435)
Ching-te-chen blue-and-white ware: porcelain with underglaze decoration in cobalt blue and with mark reading *Ta Ming Hsüan-te nien chih* within a double circle; H. 3½ in., Diam. 4 in.
1979.163

Dice Bowl with Garden Scene Illustrating the "Four Gentlemanly Pleasures" (Calligraphy, Painting, Music, and Chess)

China; Ming dynasty, Hsüan-te period (1426-1435)
Ching-te-chen blue-and-white ware: porcelain with underglaze decoration in cobalt blue and with mark reading *Ta Ming Hsüan-te nien chih* within a double circle; H. 3¾ in., Diam. 10½ in.
1979.164

Dish with Fruit and Floral Decoration

China; Ming dynasty, Hsüan-te period (1426-1435)
Ching-te-chen blue-and-white ware: porcelain with underglaze decoration in cobalt blue and with mark reading *Ta Ming Hsüan-te nien chih* within a double circle; H. 1⅞ in., Diam. 10¼ in.
1979.165

Dish with Fruit and Floral Decoration

China; Ming dynasty, Hsüan-te period (1426-1435)
Ching-te-chen blue-and-white ware: porcelain with incised decoration in reserve against underglaze cobalt blue ground and with mark reading *Ta Ming Hsüan-te nien chih*; H. 2¼ in., Diam. 11½ in.
1979.166

Bowl with Dragon and Cloud Decoration

China; Ming dynasty, Hsüan-te period (1426-1435)
Ching-te-chen blue, red, and white ware: porcelain with underglaze decoration in cobalt blue and copper red and with mark reading *Ta Ming Hsüan-te nien chih* within a double circle; H. 3 in., Diam. 6⅞ in.
1979.167

Jar with Peony Decoration

China; Ming dynasty, early 15th century (probably Hsüan-te period, 1426-1435)
Ching-te-chen blue-and-white ware: porcelain with underglaze decoration in cobalt blue; H. 9¼ in., Diam. 11¼ in.
1979.168

Large Bowl with Fruit and Floral Decoration

China; Ming dynasty, early 15th century (probably Hsüan-te period, 1426-1435)
Ching-te-chen blue-and-white ware: porcelain with underglaze decoration in cobalt blue; H. 5⅝ in., Diam. 13⅜ in.
1979.169

Lobed Vase with Stylized Floral Decoration

China; Ming dynasty, early 15th century (probably Hsüan-te period, 1426-1435)
Ching-te-chen blue-and-white ware: porcelain with underglaze decoration in cobalt blue; H. 7½ in., Diam. 5¼ in.
1979.170

Bowl with Stylized Floral Decoration

China; Ming dynasty, Ch'eng-hua period (1465-1487)
Ching-te-chen blue-and-white ware: porcelain with underglaze decoration in cobalt blue and with mark reading *Ta Ming Ch'eng-hua nien chih* within a double square; H. 2½ in., Diam. 6 in.
1979.171

Bowl with Floral Decoration

China; Ming dynasty, Ch'eng-hua period (1465-1487)
Ching-te-chen blue-and-white ware: porcelain with underglaze decoration in cobalt blue and with mark reading *Ta Ming Ch'eng-hua nien chih* within a double circle; H. 2¾ in., Diam. 6 in.
1979.172

Small Jar with Dragon and Wave Decoration

China; Ming dynasty, Ch'eng-hua period (1465-1487)
Ching-te-chen blue-and-white ware: porcelain with underglaze decoration in cobalt blue and with mark reading *Ta Ming Ch'eng-hua nien chih* within a double circle; H. 3¼ in., Diam. 4¾ in.
1979.173

Dish with Dragon and Wave Decoration

China; Ming dynasty, second half 15th century (probably Ch'eng-hua period, 1465-1487)
Ching-te-chen blue-and-white ware: porcelain with underglaze decoration in cobalt blue; H. 1½ in., Diam. 7⅞ in.
1979.174

**Wine Cup with Stylized Dragon and Floral
    Decoration**

China; Ming dynasty, Ch'eng-hua period
    (1465-1487)
Ching-te-chen *tou-ts'ai* enamelled ware:
porcelain with decoration in underglaze
cobalt blue and overglaze polychrome
enamels and with mark reading *Ta Ming
Ch'eng-hua nien chih* within a double
square; H. 1⅞ in., Diam. 2⅞ in.
1979.175

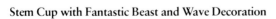

Stem Cup with Fantastic Beast and Wave Decoration

China; Ming dynasty, second half 15th century (probably Ch'eng-hua
    period, 1465-1487)
Ching-te-chen enamelled blue-and-white ware: porcelain with decoration in underglaze cobalt blue and overglaze *rouge-de-fer* enamel;
    H. 4 in., Diam. 6⅛ in.
1979.176

Dish

China; Ming dynasty, second half 15th century (probably Ch'eng-hua
    period, 1465-1487)
Ching-te-chen "sacrificial red" *(chi-hung)* ware: porcelain with speck-
led copper red glaze; H. 1⅜ in., Diam. 6½ in.
1979.177

Jar with Phoenix and Scrolling Peony Decoration in Cloisonné Style

China; Ming dynasty, late 15th century (probably Hung-chih period, 1488-1505)
Ching-te-chen *fa-hua* ware: porcelaneous stoneware with decoration in underglaze appliqué thread relief and overglaze polychrome enamels; H. 13⅞ in., Diam. 11⅞ in.
1979.178

Dish

China; Ming dynasty, Hung-chih period (1488-1505)
Ching-te-chen enamelled ware: porcelain with overglaze yellow enamel and with mark reading *Ta Ming Hung-chih nien chih* within a double circle; H. 1¾ in., Diam. 8½ in.
1979.179

Dish

China; Ming dynasty, Cheng-te period (1506-1521)
Ching-te-chen enamelled ware: porcelain with overglaze yellow enamel and with mark reading *Ta Ming Cheng-te nien chih* within a double circle; H. 1¾ in., Diam. 8⅝ in.
1979.180

Dish with Fruit and Floral Decoration

China; Ming dynasty, Cheng-te period (1506-1521)
Ching-te-chen enamelled blue-and-white ware: porcelain with underglaze decoration in cobalt blue and with overglaze yellow enamel
and with mark reading *Ta Ming Cheng-te nien chih* within a double
circle; H. 2⅛ in., Diam. 11½ in.
1979.181

Covered Water Jar with Decoration of Fish Amid Aquatic Plants

China; Ming dynasty, Chia-ching period (1522-1566)
Ching-te-chen *wu-ts'ai* enamelled ware: porcelain with decoration in
underglaze cobalt blue and overglaze polychrome enamels and with
mark reading *Ta Ming Chia-ching nien chih* within a double circle;
H. (with cover) 18½ in., Diam. 15¾ in.
1979.182 a, b

Two Plates with Decoration of Buddhist Figure Holding a Pagoda

China; Ming dynasty, early 17th century (probably T'ien-ch'i period, 1621-1627)
Blue-and-white ware: porcelain with underglaze decoration in cobalt blue; H. 1⅜ in., Diam. 8¾ in.
1979.183 and 1979.184

Beaker-shaped Vase with Squirrel and Grape Decoration

China; Ming to Ch'ing dynasty, 17th century
Ching-te-chen blue, red, and white ware: porcelain with underglaze decoration in cobalt blue and copper red; H. 39½ in., Diam. 15 in.
1979.185

Small Bowl with Partridge Decoration

China; Ch'ing dynasty, Yung-cheng period
    (1723-1735)
Ching-te-chen enamelled ware: porcelain with
    decoration in overglaze *famille rose*
    enamels and with mark reading *Ta Ch'ing
    Yung-cheng nien chih* within a double
    circle; H. 1¾ in., Diam. 3⅞ in.
1979.186

Pair of Bowls with Floral Decoration

China; Ch'ing dynasty, Yung-cheng period (1723-1735)
Ching-te-chen enamelled ware: porcelain with decoration in overglaze
    famille rose enamels and with mark reading *Ta Ch'ing Yung-cheng
    nien chih* within a double circle; H. 2½ in., Diam. 5½ in.
1979.187.1-2

Dish with Peach and Bat Decoration

China; Ch'ing dynasty, Yung-cheng period
    (1723-1735)
Ching-te-chen enamelled ware: porcelain with
    decoration in overglaze *famille rose*
    enamels and with mark reading *Ta Ch'ing
    Yung-cheng nien chih* within a double
    circle; H. 1½ in., Diam. 8⅛ in.
1979.188

Mei-p'ing Vase with Fruit and Floral Decoration

China; Ch'ing dynasty, Yung-cheng period (1723-1735)
Ching-te-chen enamelled ware: porcelain with decoration in overglaze *famille rose* enamels and with mark reading *Ta Ch'ing Yung-cheng nien chih* within a double circle; H. 13½ in., Diam. 8¾ in.
1979.189

Large Dish with Decoration of Finches on a Flowering Branch in Hsüan-te Manner

China; Ch'ing dynasty, ca. 18th century
Ching-te-chen blue-and-white ware: porcelain with underglaze decoration in cobalt blue; H. 3½ in., Diam. 19¾ in.
1979.190

KOREA

Buddha

Korea; Koryo dynasty, ca. first half 14th century
Hanging scroll; ink and color on silk; H. 38¾ in., W. 16½ in.
1979.191

Mae-byong (Mei-p'ing) Jar

Korea; Koryo dynasty, late 11th-early 12th century
Koryo celadon ware: fine-grained, light gray stoneware with celadon
    glaze; H. 15⅛ in., Diam. 9½ in.
1979.192

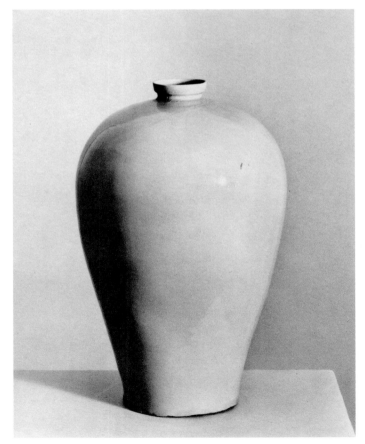

Two Sets of Foliate Bowls and Saucers

Korea; Koryo dynasty, early 12th century
Koryo celadon ware: fine-grained, light gray stoneware with celadon
  glaze; Bowls, H. 3⅝ in., Diam. 5¾ in.; Saucers, H. 1⅛ in.,
  Diam. 6¼ in.
1979.193.1-4

Bowl with Foliate Rim and Peony Decoration

Korea; Koryo dynasty, late 11th-12th century
Koryo celadon ware: fine-grained, light gray
  stoneware with incised decoration under
  celadon glaze; H. 2½ in., Diam. 7¼ in.
1979.194

Bowl with Lotus Petal Decoration

Korea; Koryo dynasty, 12th century
Koryo celadon ware: fine-grained, light gray
  stoneware with carved and incised decoration under celadon glaze; H. 3⅜ in.,
  Diam. 6¼ in.
1979.195

Storage Jar with Decoration of Crane Flying Amid Pines in Moonlight

Korea; Yi dynasty, ca. mid-18th century
Blue-and-white ware: porcelain with underglaze decoration in cobalt
blue; H. 17½ in., Diam. 13¾ in.
1979.196

Large Bottle with Lotus Decoration

Korea; Yi dynasty, ca. mid- to late 18th century
Blue-and-white ware: porcelain with underglaze decoration in cobalt
blue; H. 15½ in., Diam. 8¼ in.
1979.197

JAPAN

Standing Figure

Japan, Northern Honshu; Latest Jomon period, 1000-250 B.C.
Kamegaoka type
Gray earthenware with some black reduced areas and with traces of
red pigment on the headdress; H. 9⅞ in.
1979.198

Haniwa Figure Representing a Man with a Miter-shaped Hat

Japan, Ibaraki prefecture; Late Kofun period, 6th-7th century
Reddish buff earthenware; H. 56 in.
1979.199

Kneeling Woman

Japan; Late Nara period (710-794)
Reportedly from the five-story pagoda of
  Horyu-ji, near Nara
Clay over a wood and straw armature and
  with traces of polychromy; H. 9 in.
1979.200

Jizo Bosatsu (The Bodhisattva Kshitigarbha)

Japan; Kamakura period, between 1223 and
  1226
Cypress wood *(yosegi* or joined-block technique) with polychromy and *kirikane* (cut
  gold leaf); H. 22¾ in.
1979.202 a-e

Fudo Myo-o (The Vidyaraja Acala)

Japan; Late Heian to Kamakura period, late
  12th-early 13th century
Wood *(yosegi* or joined-block technique) with
  traces of polychromy and *kirikane* (cut
  gold leaf); H. 19¼ in.
1979.201

**Standing Male Figure, possibly Shotoku
Taishi** (573-621)
Japan; Kamakura period, 13th century
Gilt bronze; H. 9⅝ in.
1979.203 a, b

Buddha

Japan; Kamakura period, ca. 13th century
Wood (*yosegi* or joined-block technique) with
polychromy and *kirikane* (cut gold leaf);
H. 47 in.
1979.204 a, b

Nyoirin Kannon (Cintamanichakra, an Esoteric form of the
  Bodhisattva Avalokiteshvara)
Japan; Kamakura period, late 13th-early 14th century
Wood *(yosegi* or joined-block technique) with polychromy and
  kirikane (cut gold leaf); H. 19½ in.
1979.205

Pair of Koma-inu (Shinto Guardian Lions)

Japan; Kamakura to Muromachi period, 14th century
Reportedly from the Hayatama Shrine, Kumano, Wakayama
  prefecture
Wood with polychromy and gilding; H. 13½ in., L. 11½ in.
1979.206.1-2

Dainichi Nyorai (The Buddha Mahavairocana)

Japan; Kamakura period, early 13th century
Hanging scroll; ink and color on silk; H. 43½ in., W. 32⅝ in.
1979.207

Kichijoten (Shridevi)

Japan; Kamakura period, 13th century
Hanging scroll; ink and color on silk; H. 46 in.,
  W. 21¾ in.
1979.208

Blue Fudo Myo-o (The Vidyaraja Acala) **with Two Doji Attendants**

Japan; Kamakura period, ca. 1300
Hanging scroll; ink and color on silk; H. 72 in., W. 45 in.
1979.209

Shuya-do (Pavilion in a Beautiful Field)

Japan; Muromachi period, early 15th century,
 before 1437
Hanging scroll; ink and slight color on paper;
 H. 28¼ in., W. 11¼ in.
1979.210

Birds and Flowers

Attributed to Cho'oku Joki (also called Cho'oku Nyoki; active, early 16th century)
Japan; Muromachi period, late 15th-early 16th century
Hanging scroll; ink and light color on paper and with signature reading *Dai Min yushi Cho'oku Joki sha,* indicating either that he had travelled to Ming China or that he was a Chinese artist working in Japan, in which case his name would read Shu-wu Ju-ch'i; H. 28¾ in., W. 13½ in.
1979.211

Bird on a Snow-covered Plum Branch

Japan; Muromachi period, early 16th century
Hanging scroll; ink on paper; H. 54 in., W. 19¾ in.
1979.212

Poem Scroll with Bamboo

Calligraphy by Hon'ami Koetsu (1558-1637)
Painting by Tawaraya Sotatsu (active, early 17th century)
Japan; Edo period, dated to 1626
Handscroll; ink and gold on silk; H. 12⅝ in., L. 17 ft. 2½ in.
1979.214

(last section illustrated)

Birds, Ducks, and Willow Tree

Attributed to Kano Motonobu (1476-1559)
Japan; Muromachi period, ca. 1550
Possibly from Myoshin-ji, Kyoto
Sliding door *(fusuma)* panel mounted as a
    hanging scroll; ink on paper; H. 54 in.,
    W. 45 in.
1979.213

Bamboo in Mist

By Ikeno Taiga (1723-1776)
Japan; Edo period, ca. third quarter 18th century
Hanging scroll; ink and slight color on paper and
    with signature reading *Kasho;* H. 52¼ in.,
    W. 22⅞ in.
1979.215

The Four Seasons

Manner of Kano Motonobu (1476-1559)
Japan; Muromachi to Edo period; 16th-17th century
Pair of six-panel folding screens *(byobu)*; ink and light color on paper;
    H. 61 in., W. 142⅛ in. (each screen)
1979.216.1-2

Pheasants Under Cherry and Willow Trees

Iris and Mist

Attributed to Kano (originally, Watanabe)
    Ryokei (died 1645)
Japan; Edo period, first half 17th century
From the Nishi Hongan-ji collection, Kyoto
Pair of six-panel folding screens *(byobu);* ink
    and color over gold leaf on paper;
    H. 63 in., W. 143¼ in. (each screen)
1979.217.1-2

Pine and Wisteria

By Sakai Hoitsu (1761-1828)
Japan; Edo period, after 1797
Two-panel folding screen *(byobu);* ink and
    color over gold leaf on paper and with sig-
    nature reading *Hoitsu Kishin hitsu;*
    H. 60½ in., W. 61¼ in.
1979.218

Beauty Wringing Out a Towel
From the series *Fuso Ninso Juppon (Ten Examples of the Physiognomies of Women)*

By Kitagawa Utamaro (1754-1806)
Japan; Edo period, ca. 1790-1800
Woodblock print; ink, color, and mica on paper and with printed signature reading *Soken Utamaro ga;* H. 14⅞ in., W. 9⅞ in.
1979.219

Two Actors
Nakamura Konozo as Kanagawaya no Gon
Nakajima Wadaemon as Bodara no Chozaemon

By Toshusai Sharaku (active, 1794-1795)
Japan; Edo period, 1794-1795
Woodblock print; ink, color, and mica on paper and with printed signature reading *Toshusai Sharaku ga;* H. 14¾ in., W. 10 in.
1979.220

Lady and Screen

By Eishosai Choki (active, ca. 1785-1805)
Japan; Edo period, late 18th-early 19th century
Woodblock print; ink, color, and mica on paper and with printed signature reading *Choki ga;* H. 14¼ in., W. 9¾ in.
1979.222

An Actor, possibly Arashi Ryuzo

By Katsukawa Shun'ei (1762-1819)
Japan; Edo period, late 18th-early 19th century
Woodblock print; ink and color on paper and with printed signature reading *Shun'ei ga;* H. 14½ in., W. 9½ in.
1979.221

Box Cover with Phoenix, Flower, and Cloud Decoration

Japan; Late Nara period (710-794)
Gold and silver inlays in lacquer on leather *(heidatsu* technique);
    H. 3¾ in., L. 16¼ in., W. 13¼ in.
1979.223

Square Dish with Grass, Bamboo, and Wheel Decoration

Japan; Momoyama period (1568-1603)
Mino ware, Shino type: light gray stoneware with decoration in iron
    brown slip under grayish white glaze; H. 3 in., L. 8¾ in., W. 8½ in.
1979.225

Mizusashi (Water Jar for Tea Ceremony)

Japan; Momoyama to Edo period, late 16th-17th century
Iga ware: coarse-grained, light gray stoneware with impressed under-
    glaze lattice decoration; H. (with cover) 9½ in., L. 7¼ in.,
    W. 7¼ in.
1979.224 a, b

Square Dish with Bail Handle and with Decoration of Aquatic Plants

Japan; Momoyama period (1568-1603)
Mino ware, Oribe type: light gray stoneware with decoration in iron
  brown slip under white glaze and with areas splashed with copper
  green glaze; H. (with handle) 5½ in., L. 8⅛ in., W. 8⅛ in.
1979.226

Sake Bottle with Autumn Grass Decoration

Japan; Momoyama périod (1568-1603)
Mino ware, Oribe type: gray stoneware with decoration in iron brown
  slip on white slip ground under transparent glaze and with an over-
  lay of copper green glaze at the top; H. 7 in., Diam. 3¾ in.
1979.227

Dish with Combed Rim and with Decoration of Horse and Rider

Japan; Edo period, 17th century
Mino ware, Oribe type: light gray stoneware with incised decoration
  under copper green glaze; H. 2 in., Diam. 6¾ in.
1979.228

Two Mukozuke with Decoration of Autumn Grasses (Small Food
  Dishes for Tea Ceremony)

Japan; Momoyama to Edo period, late 16th-early 17th century
Karatsu ware: buff stoneware with decoration in iron brown slip
  under gray glaze; H. 4¼ in., L. (at mouth) 2¼ in., W. (at mouth)
  2¼ in.
1979.229.1-2

**Octagonal Jar with Decoration of Figures and Buildings
  in a Landscape**

Japan; Edo period, late 17th century
Arita ware, Imari type: porcelain with decoration in underglaze cobalt
  blue and overglaze polychrome enamels; H. 17⅝ in., W. 12⅜ in.
1979.231

Octagonal Jar with River Landscape Decoration

Japan; Edo period, late 17th century
Arita ware, Imari type: porcelain with underglaze decoration in cobalt
  blue; H. 20⅛ in., W. 15½ in.
1979.230

Storage Jar with Floral Decoration

Japan; Edo period, late 17th century
Arita ware, probably Imari type: porcelain with underglaze decoration
    in cobalt blue; H. 18½ in., W. 14¾ in.
1979.232

Pillow in the Shape of a Drum

Japan; Edo period, mid-18th century
Arita ware, Imari type: porcelain with decoration in overglaze
    polychrome enamels; H. 6½ in., W. 8¼ in.
1979.233

Covered Bowl with Decoration of Birds and Flowers

Japan; Edo period, mid- to late 17th century
Arita ware, Kakiemon type: porcelain with decoration in underglaze
    cobalt blue and overglaze polychrome enamels; H. (with cover)
    14⅝ in., Diam. 12 in.
1979.234 a, b

Large Bottle with Bird, Rock, and Flower Decoration

Japan; Edo period, late 17th century
Arita ware, Kakiemon type: porcelain with decoration in overglaze polychrome enamels; H. 15 ⅞ in., Diam. 8 ½ in.
1979.235

Deep Bowl with "Three Friends of Winter" Decoration (Pine, Plum, and Bamboo)

Japan; Edo period, late 17th–early 18th century
Arita ware, Kakiemon type: porcelain with decoration in overglaze polychrome enamels; H. 5 ⅛ in., Diam. 13 ¾ in.
1979.236

Deep Bowl with Decoration of Tiger, Bamboo, Flowers, and Brushwood Fence

Japan; Edo period, late 17th–early 18th century
Arita ware, Kakiemon type: porcelain with decoration in overglaze polychrome enamels and with a Johanneum mark incised into the glaze of the base; accompanied by 18th century German gilt metal mounts; H. 5 ½ in., Diam. 12 ⅞ in.
1979.237

Pair of Kara-shishi (Buddhist Guardian Lions)

Japan; Edo period, late 17th century
Arita ware, Kakiemon type: porcelain with decoration in overglaze
    polychrome enamels; H. 11⅝ in., L. 10¾ in.
1979.238.1-2

Two Female Figures

Japan; Edo period, late 17th century
Arita ware, Kakiemon type: porcelain with decoration in overglaze
    polychrome enamels; H. 15¼ in.
1979.239 and 1979.240

Seated Lady

Japan; Edo period, late 17th-early 18th century
Arita ware, Kakiemon type: porcelain with decoration in overglaze
    polychrome enamels; H. 10½ in.
1979.241

Three Mandarin Ducks (Drake, Hen, and Duckling)

Japan; Edo period, late 17th-early 18th century
Arita ware, Kakiemon type: porcelain with decoration in overglaze
    polychrome enamels, the hen with brown enamel on biscuit;
    Drake, H. 4½ in., L. 7⅝ in.; Hen, H. 4¼ in., L. 7¼ in.; Duckling,
    H. 2¾ in., L. 4¾ in.
1979.242.1-3

Gourd-shaped Bottle with Pine and Plum Decoration

Japan; Edo period, 17th century
Arita ware, Kutani style: porcelain with decoration in overglaze
    polychrome enamels; H. 10⅜ in., Diam. 5¾ in.
1979.243

Large Bottle with Floral Decoration

Japan; Edo period, mid-17th century
Arita ware, Kutani style: porcelain with decoration in over-
    glaze polychrome enamels; H. 17 in., Diam. 10 in.
1979.244

High-footed Bowl with Leaf and Stylized Floral Decoration

Japan; Edo period, mid- to late 17th century
Kutani ware, Green Kutani type: porcelain with decoration in over-
    glaze polychrome enamels; H. 4 in., Diam. 12¼ in.
1979.245

High-footed Dish with Floral Decoration

Japan; Edo period, 17th century
Kutani ware: porcelain with decoration in overglaze polychrome
    enamels; H. 4 in., Diam. 11½ in.
1979.246

Plate with "Checkerboard" Decoration

Japan; Edo period, late 17th-early 18th century
Kutani ware, Green Kutani type: porcelain with decoration in overglaze polychrome enamels and with underglaze mark reading *fuku*
  on the base; H. 2¾ in., Diam. 13¼ in.
1979.247

Plate with Chrysanthemum Decoration

Japan; Edo period, late 17th century
Arita ware, Nabeshima type: porcelain with decoration in underglaze
  cobalt blue and overglaze polychrome enamels; H. 2 in., Diam.
  7⅞ in.
1979.249

Dish with Decoration of Flowering Cherry Tree and Curtains

Japan; Edo period, late 17th century
Arita ware, Nabeshima type: porcelain with decoration in underglaze
  cobalt blue and with a band of iron brown glaze at the top and a
  band of celadon type glaze in the center; H. 1⅝ in., Diam. 7¾ in.
1979.248

Plate with Pomegranate Decoration

Japan; Edo period, late 17th century
Arita ware, Nabeshima type: porcelain with decoration in underglaze
    cobalt blue and overglaze polychrome enamels; H. 3⅜ in., Diam.
    11⅜ in.
1979.250

Chatsubo (Tea Jar) with Decoration of Rock, Bamboo, and Crows

By Nonomura Ninsei (active, mid-17th century)
Japan; Edo period, mid-17th century
Kyoto ware: light gray stoneware with decoration in overglaze poly-
    chrome enamels and with a seal reading *Ninsei* impressed on the
    unglazed base; H. 12 in., Diam. 9½ in.
1979.251

Deep Bowl with Reticulated Rim and Decoration of Mist and Grasses

By Ogata Kenzan (1663-1743)
Japan; Edo period, first half 18th century
Kyoto ware: buff stoneware with decoration in underglaze slips and
    overglaze polychrome enamels and with underglaze signature read-
    ing *Kenzan* on the base; H. 4⅞ in., Diam. 7½ in.
1979.252

PROMISED GIFTS

Parvati

South India, Tamil Nadu; Chola period, 11th
    century
Bronze; H. 21¼ in.
Promised gift of Mrs. John D. Rockefeller 3rd

The Bodhisattva Avalokiteshvara

Nepal; 8th-9th century
Gilt bronze; H. 13¼ in.
Promised gift of Mrs. John D. Rockefeller 3rd

Uma-Maheshvara-murti (Shiva and Parvati)

Nepal; 9th-10th century
Brownish stone with traces of gold leaf;
    H. 16 in.
Promised gift of Mrs. John D. Rockefeller 3rd

Crowned Buddha Seated in Meditation and Sheltered by Mucilinda

Thailand or Cambodia; Khmer style, 12th century
Gray stone; H. 42½ in.
Promised gift of Mrs. John D. Rockefeller 3rd

Stele Depicting the Buddhas Shakyamuni and Prabhutaratna

China; Six Dynasties period, Northern Ch'i, ca. 575
Ting-chou School
White marble; H. 24½ in.
Promised gift of Mrs. John D. Rockefeller 3rd

Standing Male Figure

Cambodia; Angkor period, second half 11th century
Style of Baphuon
Reddish buff sandstone; H. 50 in.
Promised gift of Arthur Ross

Horse

China; T'ang dynasty, ca. 8th century
"Three-color" *(san-ts'ai)* ware: white earthenware with variegated lead glaze; H. 23 in.
Promised gift of Mrs. John D. Rockefeller 3rd